NUTS AND BOLTS
FOR THE NEW AUTHOR
AND THE NEW PUBLISHER
MADE SIMPLE

What You Need To Know To Jump-Start And Sustain

Your Writing/Publishing Business

DR. ROSIE MILLIGAN

Published and Distributed by:
Professional Publishing House
1425 W. Manchester Ave., Suite B
Los Angeles, California 90047
www.professionalpublishinghouse.com
Drrosie@aol.com
(323) 750-3592

Cover design: Jay De Vance, III

First printing: August 2012
10 9 8 7 6 5 4 3 2 1

ISBN: 978-0-9771082-4-4

Library of Congress Control Number: 2012913312

DEDICATION

To all the mothers and fathers of "Book Babies," may
you nourish your book baby well so that it may grow
and become something great.

ABOUT THE AUTHOR

Dr. Rosie Milligan, professional business consultant, author, financial/estate planner and Ph.D. in Business Administration, has always been an achiever. Every career or business in which she has been involved includes helping others accomplish their goals in life. Her motto, "Erase No, Step Over Can't and Move Forward With Life," has been a motivating influence for hundreds to whom she has been mentor and role model.

A mother of three entrepreneurs: an M.D., a cosmetologist, and a book and herb store owner, Dr. Milligan lectures nationally on economic empowerment, management diversity in the workplace, and male/female relationships. Her books *Starting a Business Made Simple* and *Getting out of Debt Made Simple*, have helped many across the country. She is the author of seventeen books. She has co-authored four books with her sister, Attorney Clara Hunter King, *What You Need To Know Before You Start A Business, Departing This Life Preparations, How To Write A Book Made Simple, and ABC's On How To Prepare Your Manuscript For Editing, Formatting, And Printing, and What You Need to Know Before You Get Hitched.*

A successful motivational speaker and trainer, she has appeared on numerous television and radio shows, such as *The Sally Jesse Raphael Show* in New York; *A.M. Philadelphia*; *Evening Exchange* in Washington, D.C., *Marilyn Kagan Show* in Los Angeles, and she is a regular guest on Stevie Wonder's KJLH Radio. She is the host of a weekly live Internet talk show and she is founder and director of "Black Writers on Tour."

TABLE OF CONTENTS

PREFACE

This book provides answers to the most frequently asked questions by self-published and mainstream published authors. In my "Dear Dr. Rosie" column for a book review magazine, I received numerous emails with questions regarding the publishing business. In this book, I am providing answers to fifteen of the most asked questions of "Dear Dr. Rosie." The questions and answers are critical to the success of any author, whether self-published or mainstream published.

The publishing industry has changed drastically within the last ten years. Numerous bookstores have closed. Mainstream publishers are taking fewer risks with new authors. More people seem eager to write now than ever before. Writers are no longer willing to sit on the sideline, waiting and begging mainstream publishers to accept their work for publishing. They are starting their own publishing companies. However, many are not knowledgeable about the business. They make many mistakes and exhaust most of their finances before they learn the "Nuts & Bolts" of the book business. Writing this book has a two-fold purpose: To impress upon the writer that book publishing is a business and must be treated as such. I would recommend that the new writer and publisher read *What You Should Know Before You Start A Business,* a much-needed tool written by my sister attorney Clara Hunter King and me.

Numerous distributors have closed also, leaving author/publisher to find new ways of getting books to the people who want to buy their book. The difference between the successful author/publisher and the unsuccessful author/publisher is that the successful author/publisher has availed themselves to knowledge on how to start and manage a successful business, and they understand the importance of a good marketing plan for their business. Although I answer a question asked regarding the importance of a marketing plan in this book, you would gain a more in-depth knowledge by reading my eBook, *Developing A Marketing Plan For Your Book Made Simple.*

Please know that you can have a successful business as a writer/publisher, but you *must* acquire knowledge about the business.

DO I NEED A MARKETING PLAN FOR MY BOOK?

DO I NEED A MARKETING PLAN FOR MY BOOK?

Dear Dr. Rosie,

I recently self-published a nonfiction book. However, I am running into roadblocks when attempting to obtain a national distributor and trying to get my book in the small press department of Barnes & Noble. Both are asking for a marketing plan, and I don't have a clue as to what they really want from me. What is a marketing plan and why are they requesting it? Please help!

Dear Author,

You are not alone in your dilemma. A marketing plan is a crucial component of a business plan. An author must see their book as a business venture and not a simple hobby. Every self-publisher should have a business plan.

A business plan is a description of your venture. It is a management tool that helps you achieve success much easier. The marketing plan is a blueprint of a business. Consider purchasing a book on marketing plans or check one out at your local library.

Distributors as well as many bookstores are now requesting a marketing plan before considering carrying an author's book. They have legitimate reasons for doing so. A marketing plan in simple language is the strategies used to drive the intended buyers to purchase your product. Your book is your product.

There are thousands of books released every year and what all books have in common is a need for shelf space in both the bookstores as well as space in a distributor's warehouse. Bookstores and distributors have space concerns; therefore, they are driven by a "book demand" when selecting a product to sell.

A marketing plan tells the booksellers how you plan to create demand for your book. Bookstores and distributors are interested in books that have the greatest selling potential. Below are some low-budget marketing strategies:

1. Mail notices announcing your book to all your relatives, friends and associates.

2. Send a press release about your book to 25 book-stores, nationwide per week.

3. Host an unveiling book party within 30 days after your book is released and invite all your friends and relatives, nationwide.

4. Ask your pastor (minister, etc.) if you can have a book signing at your church.

5. Ask your sorority/fraternity group to host a book signing for you.

6. Ask permission to hold a book signing at your work place or at the schools you've attended.

7. Contact your local library and ask to present a lecture and provide a book signing.

8. Visit local bookstores, meet the owner/manager and ask if they will host a book signing for you.

9. Look up book clubs on the Internet and send them a notice about your book. Offer to speak at their book club meeting.

10. Offer schools, charity groups, sororities, etc., an opportunity to sell your book as a fundraising venue. Offer them a 20% discount on all retail sales.

11. Offer your book as a give-away on local radio stations.

12. Have post cards and/or bookmarkers made of your book cover to mail or distribute at bookstores.

13. Have your friends to host book parties at their homes for you.

14. Notify schools that you have attended or graduated from and let them know about your book. Ask to come and speak and sign your book.

15. Send information about your book to college bookstores.

16. Notify friends of your parents and your children's friends' parents about your book.

17. Ask your local newspapers to do a book review.

18. Send your book with a press release to local talk show hosts, including ten questions that you would like the host to ask you.

19. Contact your local cable television shows regarding being a guest on one of their upcoming shows, they need good guest. Do not forget to ask for referrals.

20. Join a toastmasters group if you have a fear of speaking in front of people.

21. Exhibit your book at local expos and book fairs.

Hopefully, this information will help you fill in the blanks of the form sent to you by distributors and bookstores. Please remember that bookstores are not the only avenue for selling your books and do not overlook the many large churches that have bookstores and book fairs. Volunteer to speak at your local clubs and community functions. You should develop a basic web site, including a homepage with your book cover, a book synopsis of the book or what people are saying, where to buy, how to contact you and an e-commerce account so that clients may purchase your book with their credit/debit cards.

Good luck with your new book.

I'VE LOST ALL EXCITEMENT ABOUT MY BOOK. I AM SUFFERING FROM "BOOK BLUES." DO MAINSTREAM AUTHORS HAVE SIMILAR PROBLEMS?

I'VE LOST ALL EXCITEMENT ABOUT MY BOOK. I AM SUFFERING FROM "BOOK BLUES." DO MAINSTREAM AUTHORS HAVE SIMILAR PROBLEMS?

Dear Dr. Rosie,

I've lost all excitement for my book. In fact, I feel as though I am suffering from "book blues." I was so sure that I would sell 50,000 books my first year. I have sold 2,500 books for the first year. I am depressed. Do mainstream authors have similar problems? Please help!

Dear Author,

I hear you loud and clear. You are voicing the sentiments of hundreds of writers experiencing "postpartum" book blues. Many authors' book sales expectations are totally unrealistic for their first book, especially if the author is not nationally known and not a public speaker.

And yes, mainstream writers do have similar problems. Remember, there are only a few blockbuster authors. Many mainstream authors don't sell 10,000 books a year. And often, books by mainstream-published authors end up on the remainder list before they are six months to one-year-old. (Remainders are books that publishers are no longer promoting. These books are sold to wholesalers for $1 to $4, even hardcover books).

In many ways, publishing your first book is like having a baby. At first, new mothers are excited, expecting the baby to be well-behaved and to sleep through the night. But after a while, the excitement wears off once a mother realizes it involves more work than she anticipated.

For a new author, a well thought-out business plan with a strong marketing plan is crucial. As a consultant, I have reviewed many business plans and most of them have inadequate marketing strategies, which are the lifeline of a book. As a writer, you must see your book as a business. You should develop your marketing plan, accordingly.

Sometimes, authors do not know how to measure

success as it relates to book sales. Success should not be based on what other authors tell you about their book sales. If you sold 2,500 books in 12 months, you did well, especially if you didn't have a marketing plan, and you are not an experienced self-promoter.

You can alleviate your frustration about your book by getting back into the business of promoting your book the right way by developing a well-designed marketing plan.

You should consider collaborating with other authors to arrange book-signing venues and share expenses. Start setting goals and consider inexpensive and innovative ways to achieve them. Look at the time and money necessary to make your goals a reality, and periodically re-evaluate your methods. Set targets for the number of books that you want to sell to wholesalers, bookstores and retail buyers.

Get back in the race, and run it with renewed vigor. Keep your book alive and well¾after all, its your dream.

WHY DO I NEED A STORY EDITOR AND/OR A COPY EDITOR FOR MY NOVEL? WHICH IS MORE IMPORTANT?

WHY DO I NEED A STORY EDITOR AND / OR A COPY EDITOR FOR MY NOVEL? WHICH IS MORE IMPORTANT?

Dear Dr. Rosie,

I am a fiction writer. I've consulted with a publishing packaging company to assist me with publishing my book. They said that my book is good, but it needs to be story edited and copy edited. Why do I need to pay for two edits? Which is more important?

Dear Author,

Yes, it's definitely important to pay the extra cost for two editors. The question you asked is one I hear frequently; so I will explain what each editor does with a manuscript. The story editor is concerned with things such as: pacing (Does the story move along well? Does the reader have to re-read to make sense of what is happening in the story?); character development (Can the reader connect with or feel the characters? Are the characters believable? Are you introducing too many characters at the same time?); conflict (Is conflict or tension introduced early enough in the story? Does the reader get a sense of tension building and is the reader motivated to keep reading to see the resolution?); verb tense consistency (Is the writer consistent in the use of the present or past tense?); point of view (Is the story told in the first or the third person? Is the story being told by the writer, a narrator or the main character?); Am I using the art of 'Show vs. Tell'? Do I have language dissonance regarding the type of characters that I am portraying? For example, do I have a scientist speaking in street talk, or a street person speaking like a college professor? If so, there should be a logical reason, such as the scientist pulled himself up by his bootstraps from the streets, or the street person self-educated himself. Do I plant a macguffin (plot device)—which is a goal or desire or yearning, which will fuel the plot?

Are you telling the reader or are you showing the reader the drama? Can the reader feel what is happening?

Does the reader get caught up in the story? Am I involving the emotions of my reader so that he will root for my main character? Am I using a compelling situation? Have I layered my plot and my subplots? Do I use stilted versus conversational dialogue? Do I introduce my back story too soon?

This is only the beginning. There is much more to what a story editor looks for when editing a novel, but the input of such a professional is incalculably valuable to any writer, whether it is their first novel or their tenth.

The copy editor is mainly concerned with spelling, grammar, and sentence structure. This editor makes certain that all of your words are spelled correctly and that there is verb agreement throughout the story. A good copy editor will check for sentence fragments, run-on sentences or paragraphs that run on too long, as well as making sure that adjectives and adverbs are used sparingly and correctly.

I am inspired by writers who continue to seek knowledge and refine their craft in order to give readers their best work. I must warn you that most people don't know the difference. Therefore, an editor may tell you he/she does both, but be wary of such claims. A good story editor does not want to concern herself with copy editing and vice versa. I would suggest that you choose editors through referrals from a prudent person in the industry.

I AM TIRED OF THE REJECTION LETTERS. SHOULD I SELF-PUBLISH OR KEEP TRYING MAINSTREAM PUBLISHERS?

I AM TIRED OF THE REJECTION LETTERS. SHOULD I SELF-PUBLISH OR KEEP TRYING MAINSTREAM PUBLISHERS?

Dear Dr. Rosie,

I am tired of having my manuscript rejected. I am considering the self-publishing route. But should I keep trying to get it published with a mainstream house or should I self-publish?

Dear Author,

This question requires a long answer and some soul-searching on your part. In order to decide if self-publishing is the right route; you must first decide what your motivation is. Here are some questions you might ask yourself to help decide whether to self-publish or not:

- Are you interested in sharing your knowledge?

- Do you want the personal satisfaction of being published?

- Are you seeking credibility for your work?

- Are you a speaker with an audience and will your book be an additional profit-making opportunity?

- Do you want fame?

- Will a book advance your career?

- Are you seeking to make writing a new career and want to quit your job?

A word of advice: Don't quit your day job, or at least not yet. The problem you're encountering lies not in the fact that you don't have an agent to represent you or a publisher for your book. The real issue lies in the fact that you've failed to understand clearly or identify what your motives are for publishing.

When you have been repeatedly rejected, your only option may be to self-publish, if you want to see your work in print. Remember, there is nothing wrong with being a self-published author. These authors once self-published their books:

- The late E. Lynn Harris *Invisible Life*

- John Grisham *A Time to Kill*

- Robert T. Kiyosaki *Rich Dad, Poor Dad*

- Jack Canfield and Mark Victor Hanson *Chicken Soup for the Soul*

Writing a book and self-publishing a book requires different skills. Writing is an art, self-publishing is a business venture.

Whether your book is published by a mainstream publisher or self-published, you should consider your book a "business." Even if you get a mainstream publisher, you should still view your book as a business, just not one that involves only you. You must get involved in marketing your book to make it a success. If you self-publish, you are in business for yourself and for the most part, you're in it all by yourself.

It's important that you ask yourself these questions:

- Do you have the entrepreneurial spirit?

- Are you a self-starter?

- Are you highly motivated?

- Do you have thick skin or will you be crushed when others reject or criticize your work?

- Are you willing to take risks?

- Can you afford to spend thousands of dollars to get your book published?

- Can you put the profits from the book back into the business? If not, you may not be able to reprint your book when it sells out.

Unfortunately, that has happened to too many self-published writers.

They take money from their household budget or living expenses to publish their books and replace the money with funds from book sales. They can't afford to plow money back into their books and aren't able to follow through. That is not a good practice.

The book business is like any other business; you must have start-up capital. If your book is successful, oftentimes major publishers will take an interest in your work and want to publish your book. However, you may just want to reject their offer if you already have a following, a website, and a great distribution.

Whether your goal is to get published by a large publisher or to self-publish, you should obtain the services of a professional book consultant to help you produce a quality product. Find a copy editor and a proofreader. Do not edit your book yourself. Do not have a friend do it for you unless your friend is a professional editor. Even though your friend may be an English teacher, she may not be good at editing a book.

If your book is fiction, you should consider having it story-edited as well. Your cover should be designed by a professional graphic artist or designer, and make sure you have your book professionally formatted. Packaging is a very important aspect in the sale of your book. The format of your book must be reader-friendly. A point size that is too large is as hard on the eye as one that's too small. A 12-point type size is good. Ideally, you shouldn't go below an 11-point type size.

Today's technology with on-demand printing, the internet, social media, blogging, literary services, and professional book packaging services have made the job easier. Many on-demand publishers also provided book fulfillment services.

These services make self-publishing more attractive since the author doesn't have to bother with packing, shipping, or collecting money for book sales. Some on-demand printers, however, do not bill or collect money. They may only own the warehouse and ship books to customers. They do charge a warehouse fee and shipping charges.

What you are left with when using these services is marketing your book and doing what you love the most—writing.

CAN PUBLIC SPEAKING INCREASE AN AUTHOR'S BOOK SALES?

CAN PUBLIC SPEAKING INCREASE AN AUTHOR'S BOOK SALES?

Dear Dr. Rosie,

How important are public speaking classes for authors?

Dear Author,

For many people, one of their most common fears is speaking in front of an audience. I think any author who has mastered the art of public speaking has an advantage over one who has not.

While there are a number of courses offered in public speaking, I recommend joining Toastmasters International. There, you will learn how to cut to the chase and get your point across quickly. You'll learn how to respond in an impromptu situation and deal with circumstances where speaking involves time constraints. You'll learn techniques from professional speakers, and Toastmasters International has experts who can evaluate your skills.

In most public speaking courses, students are asked to speak in front of an audience at least every other week; each speech is critiqued and evaluated by the instructor. Participants are judged based on the timing of the speech, voice intonation and gestures. A public-speaking class can help writers gain more confidence, which can help increase book sales. On several occasions, I have been asked to speak by nonprofit organizations whose budgets did not allow an honorarium. My question usually is, "How many people do you normally have attending these events?" If the answer is a hundred or more, then it's worth participating. In some cases, I have walked away with $500 to $3,000 in book sales, and $1,000 to $5,000 for a speaker's fee.

Being a good communicator is beneficial no matter what career you choose. You don't have to be a speaker to sell books. Authors who are good public speakers will sell more books, even if they don't have an established name.

AS AN AUTHOR, DO I NEED AN INTERNET PRESENCE? CAN I MARKET ON THE INTERNET? WHAT DOES IT COST TO HAVE A WEB SITE DEVELOPED?

AS AN AUTHOR, DO I NEED AN INTERNET PRESENCE? CAN I MARKET ON THE INTERNET? WHAT DOES IT COST TO HAVE A WEB SITE DEVELOPED?

Dear Dr. Rosie,

Just how important is it for self-published authors to have an Internet presence and what are ways I can market my books on the Internet? Lastly, what does it cost for a basic web site?

Dear Author,

You have many great questions, my dear. I will address each one individually. First of all, the Internet can be a powerful tool when you make maximum use of its applications. It is a great way for self-published authors to create the "funk" for books. When I say, "Create the book funk," I mean make sure your book is in everybody's face—guerrilla marketing is what I am talking about. With the Internet, you can promote your book to book clubs, get permission from other sites to link to your website, or write articles for websites and mention your book as part of your byline for the article.

One of the most powerful new tools to promote your book is on Internet radio talk shows. Internet talk radio is a global market. Recently, I listened to the Dr. Maxine Show on www.maxineshow.com and host Dr. Maxine Thompson, was interviewing an author from Paris. The listening audience was able to call in and talk to the host and the author. This is clearly a revolutionary Internet break-through for books.

I have an Internet talk show, www.drrosie.com, every Tuesday from 10 to 11AM PST (live talk with call-in). I have interviewed authors nationwide and their book sales has increased substantially .

Internet radio talk show programs can involve an author in Los Angeles interviewed by a radio station in New York. The interview is conducted via telephone or

Skype. The difference is a local radio station can only reach a limited audience due to its signal. However, most radio station's talk shows are now on the World Wide Web. When you are on a radio talk show, traditional or the Internet, you should notify your clientele and database via emailing or calling them.

Anyone who has access to the Internet can listen to and participate in Internet talk radio. With the Internet, authors can promote their books with a low budget, or practically no budget and get national and international publicity. You can develop an Internet and website presence for less than $60 per month. To keep costs down and control your image, you should manage your own website.

The fee for building a basic web site should be no more than $350.00. You do not need to pay a webmaster to manage your web site. It's better to pay a webmaster a consulting fee to have them teach you how to manage your site. Microsoft FrontPage and Dreamweaver are good programs for building your web site.

A basic web site presentation should include:

1. A home page including your book cover and publisher information

2. An author's picture and biography

3. Any press release excerpts or book reviews

4. A book-signing/speaking schedule

5. An order form and information about where to buy your book

6. E-commerce because being able to accept credit cards can increase your book sales

You can also market to booksellers on the Internet. A serious author should spend at least two hours a day marketing online. You can find book clubs on the Internet. Many book clubs are interviewing authors via speaker telephone, Skype, etc. With social media such as: Facebook and Twitter, you can frequently post excerpts and other information about your book. You can place an online dialogue talking about your book on YouTube.

So listen up! Remember, the Internet is to an author what a tree is to a branch¾it allows you to grow.

You must create the "funk," driving people to your web site by any means necessary via emailing, twittering, and facebooking, and asking friends to email their friends and associates. REMEMBER, IF YOU DON'T ASK, YOU WON'T GET.

I AM TORN WITH THE DECISION TO
SELF-PUBLISH OR TO GO MAINSTREAM.

I AM TORN WITH THE DECISION TO SELF-PUBLISH OR TO GO MAINSTREAM.

Dear Dr. Rosie,

I self-published my first novel and sold 5,000 copies in eight months. I want to sell it to a publisher, but am somewhat torn by my decision because many publishers initially rejected my manuscript. I feel that they will want it now because it is selling well. I am a sought-after speaker and have been featured in many newspaper articles. What should I do?

Dear Author,

You suffer from a problem many self-published writers sometimes experience. First, you should be congratulated for pursuing your dream of seeing your book in print. You have demonstrated your determination by selling 5,000 books.

The sale of 5,000 books in eight months tells me that there's a market for your work. The fact that you have been featured in newspapers attests to your sales ability. Your sales and marketing savvy is what gets an editor's attention. Your resentment about previously being rejected by publishers is understandable. However, the trend in mainstream publishing today is to favor self-published authors who have an established track record.

Readers tend to follow authors they like, and they often ask, "When is your next book coming out?" It should encourage you to know that many popular mainstream authors were originally self-published and bestsellers. Here are a few examples:

Author	Book Title	Published In	Title Reissued by
E. Lynn Harris	*Invisible Life*	1992	Anchor Books, 1994
Omar Tyree	*Flyy Girl*	1993	Simon & Schuster, 1996
Franklin White	*Fed Up With the Fanny*	1996	Simon & Schuster, 1998
Kimberla Lawson Roby	*Behind Closed Doors*	1997	Black Classic Press, 1997
Timmothy McCann	*Until*	1997	Avon, 1999
Evelyn Palfrey	*The Price of Passion*	1997	Pocket Books, 2000
Parry Brown	*The Shirt Off His Back*	1998	Strivers Row, 2001
Tajuana (TJ) Butler	*Sorority Sisters*	1998	Villard, 2000
Camika Spencer	*When All Hell Breaks Loose*	1998	Random House, 1999
Karen Quiones Miller	*Satin Doll*	2000	Simon & Schuster, 2001

At times, self-publishing can be a stepping stone for authors who want to be picked up by mainstream publishers. From your letter, it seems that you have wanted to be published by a major publisher rather than take the self-publishing route. So, go for your dream and feel good about it. Remember, it's very difficult to get a first novel published. A novelist's career depends on showing everyone, from the publishers, to the media, to the readers, that your first book has merit. Your book has passed the test. So get the show on the road and go for your dreams.

I AM AN AUTHOR/BOOKSTORE OWNER WHO IS BECOMING DISCOURAGED. WHAT CAN I DO?

I AM AN AUTHOR/BOOKSTORE OWNER WHO IS BECOMING DISCOURAGED. WHAT CAN I DO?

Dear. Dr. Rosie,

I am an author and a bookstore owner who is becoming discouraged with the book business. If many independent black bookstores are struggling and closing their doors, what is the future for black authors? I'm about to give up. Tell me what to do.

Dear Author/Bookstore owner:

You are looking at both sides of the business. I think I can help you since I am an author and also a bookstore owner. One thing I think you should consider is, "How you view your world, determines how you view the world," advice that I offer in my book *Milliganisms: Motivational Quotations & How Comes.* Your own world seems bleak; therefore, you see the world that way.

The terrorist attack on September 11, 2001, the war in Iraq, Hurricane Katrina, labor contracts to the prison industry complex, and outsourcing of labor outside the country has had a negative effect on the economy. As a result, we must rethink our strategies for doing business. We must hone our marketing strategies so that we can continue to build our businesses. As an author, you will have to be creative and resourceful in marketing yourself and your book. Here are some things you can do:

1. Send bookmarks or postcards with your book cover on it to bookstore owners.

2. Send a letter of inquiry to book clubs asking them to consider choosing your book for discussion. Include your media kit, which should include a press release, biography, your photo, clips of any press you have received and a copy of your book.

3. Make sure you are on the Internet with a Web presence.

4. Become a toastmaster and join a speaker's club.

5. Showcase your books at expos, cultural fairs, literary conferences and events.

6. Read the newspaper and listen to the news for story ideas relating to your book and submit press releases or articles to be considered for publication.

7. Seek out hosts of broadcast or Internet radio talk shows and ask to be a guest. Send the host a press kit.

8. There are local cable television programs in most cities. Seek them out. What they usually all have in common is that they need guests. You need them and they need you. Donate books to local radio stations to give away as promotional items.

9. Attend writers' conferences and learn more about how to market your book. Develop relationships with people who can help you. The bottom line is that you must be creative and try new ways of marketing.

Now let me address your concerns as a bookstore owner. I have had great success with my bookstore. Let me share with you some of the reasons why my business has grown. I've created an atmosphere in my bookstore of belonging to the community. I seek their input. When our customers enter the door, we immediately go up to assist them. We show them new products or new book arrivals. We also keep them abreast of current issues for topics of discussion. Clients love to share their views and ideas, especially in troubled times, and they love to be in the presence of positive people.

Never neglect customers. Provide fast, efficient service; help customers with purchases; talk to them and offer advice about available books; work the floor; and go the extra mile to provide them with the books and information they request.

It is important that you create profit centers within your store. You will find it a little difficult just to sell books. Also try to carry popular books by non-black authors on subjects such as self-help, psychology, and finance. Add a selection of Spanish books if there is an audience for them.

We sell vitamins, greeting cards, oils, and hair care and spa products. We also provide fax, copy, and laminating services. Find what works for you and do it!

AS AN AUTHOR, HOW CAN I MAKE EXPOS AND CONFERENCES WORK FOR ME?

AS AN AUTHOR, HOW CAN I MAKE EXPOS AND CONFERENCES WORK FOR ME?

Dear Dr. Rosie,

I have attended many expo venues and writers' conferences to sell my book. I was always, however, disappointed with my book sales. I have always heard that networking is important, but it has not worked for me. Am I missing something?

Dear Author,

Yes, you are. The relationships you build by networking can open many doors for you, but networking and selling books are completely different.

Expos, exhibitions and writer's conferences are avenues to get exposure and make connections. The common mistake that authors make when exhibiting is remaining stuck at their booths. They get so involved selling books that they fail to use the networking opportunities.

Most times, authors bring too many books, and they feel pressured to sell. This causes them to lose sight of networking. Set a realistic goal. Add up your expense for the venue and aim to cover most of it. If it cost $800 for booth space, transportation, lodging and food, divide the retail price of your book into total expense. The result will tell you how many sales you need. If your book retails at $15, you need to sell 53 books. If you sell 50 books at a one-day event where you are not the keynote speaker or presenter, you have done exceptionally well. As a keynote speaker or presenter at an event with a large attendance, you can sell hundreds of books.

When someone tells you to expect 10,000 to attend an event, do not let that override common sense about how many books you can sell. Most attendees will not even come down the aisle where you exhibit.

To maximize your networking potential, bring someone to help you manage your booth and give you some free time. You might also consider sharing a booth with another author or bookstore vendor.

Here are a few more networking tips:

1. If you wish to meet someone, if possible, have someone who knows him or her to introduce you.

2. Give them your card, but more importantly, get theirs.

3. When following up, remind them where you met and what you talked about. After all, they probably talked with many other people at the same place.

Finally, networking opportunities may outweigh the sales potential of an event. You can meet people who can unlock doors for you or people who have influence with people who can open doors for you. These elements are keys to success for any author.

I HAVE SELF-PUBLISHED THREE BOOKS. IT IS HARD FOR ME TO KEEP ALL THREE BOOKS IN PRINT. WHAT ARE MY OPTIONS?

I HAVE SELF-PUBLISHED THREE BOOKS. IT IS HARD FOR ME TO KEEP ALL THREE BOOKS IN PRINT. WHAT ARE MY OPTIONS?

Dear Dr. Rosie,

I am a self-published author who has published three books. As a speaker, I have been able to create an even greater demand for my books. However, I cannot afford to keep more than one book in print at a time. I am extremely frustrated. Can you offer any suggestions?

Dear Author,

Many authors find themselves in this position because conventional printing methods are cost-prohibitive when printing smaller quantities. For example, if you wanted to print just 500 copies through conventional printing, it would cost approximately $8.00 per copy for a 250-300 page trade paperback. The challenge is that most books retail in the $12.95-$14.95 range, so there is no room for profit. You would have to print 1,000-plus books to get a better price break on printing costs.

However, a revolutionary breakthrough called on-demand printing can be the solution for many self-published authors and small publishers. On-demand printing allows the author to print only books that are ordered. Your book is put into the on-demand printer's system, and booksellers simply order the quantity they need. Books are printed within 48-72 hours and shipped to fulfill the order. That means you only pay for the books that are actually ordered. The best part of on-demand printing is that the costs for low quantities are very reasonable. Though costs will vary by company, the average cost for printing 1 to 100 books through this method is approximately $4.50 per book. Using traditional printing methods, an author would have to print 1,000 to 1,500 books to get costs down to $2.50 per book.

On-demand printing saves money in other ways. First, the author does not have to keep books in storage.

Second, some on-demand publishers are responsible for collection, so that the author does not have to run from bookstore to bookstore, performing the duties of a collection agent. Additionally, some on-demand printing companies have distribution programs, making your book available through large national book distributors.

Most print-on-demand companies do charge a setup fee, usually about $300. After that, the only costs are for the actual printing. There may be additional costs for the distribution and marketing programs. However, any costs are small compared to the benefits provided by on-demand printing.

All in all, on-demand printing helps the self-published author return to what he or she loves: writing, speaking, and marketing.

DO I NEED A BOOK DISTRIBUTOR?

DO I NEED A BOOK DISTRIBUTOR?

Dear Dr. Rosie,

I recently self-published my first book. I have great marketing skills and have made contact with a number of people in the radio, television, and print media. I've got the hookup to get plenty exposure for my book. My concern is that I have to give major distributors a 55% discount on my book. Doc, this just doesn't seem fair play to me. I wrote the book, paid for the cost of the book, and am doing my own marketing. Why should I give such a high discount? Should I just sell my book on Amazon.com, etc. or give it up and pay the price?

Dear Author,

You are not alone in asking these questions. Discounts given to major distributors are concerns for most new writers. Let me tell you why you might just have to suck it up.

Good book distribution is the key to your book's success. I acquired a client who had been published by a small independent publisher, but had not obtained national distribution for his book. The publisher printed 2,000 books. The author even got a guest spot on Oprah. I met him six months after his television appearance, and he still had 1,500 books in storage. Why? Because he had no major distribution.

Most new authors want to go after national radio, television, and print media attention. My advice has always been that publicity should not precede distribution. When audiences hear you on the radio, see you on the television, or read about your book in print, they are moved and want to buy your book¾now. If they go to a major chain store that store would order from a large distributor, not from you. Also remember that for many small cities, large chain bookstores are the only ones available.

The book industry is a business where profits are shared by many. In addition to the 55% discount required by major distributors, you are also required to pay for the freight, and you must have a book return policy for over-stocked books.

Let's look at the role of the distributor. Distributor's wholesale books to bookstores to which they give a 40-50% discount. Even if you sell directly to bookstores, they get a 40% discount. Everyone who participates in your book's sale makes money.

Most online booksellers require a 55% discount as well, and you still pay for freight. Welcome to the world of WOW! Bookselling is an industry where only the strong (and the ones with business savvy) survive. Still, it can be quite rewarding if you understand the business of books.

Bottom line, you cannot sell your books by yourself. Remember that 45% of a lot is still more than 1000% of a little. So get busy and make your dream happen!

HOW DO I HAVE A SUCCESSFUL

BOOK SIGNING?

HOW DO I HAVE A SUCCESSFUL

BOOK SIGNING?

Dear Dr. Rosie,

I am a self-published author, and as part of my promotional efforts, I have scheduled book signings at several stores. Although I've had over ten signings, none have been successful. I've done four local signings and six out of town. No matter where I have been, only a handful of people showed up¾most of whom just happened to be in the store at the time. I have lost so much money traveling to other cities and selling just ten or so books. Are the bookstores doing something wrong? I am so frustrated that I'm ready to throw in the towel.

Dear Author,

There are few experiences more disappointing for an author than to be sitting behind a table, surrounded by books hoping that someone will make a purchase.

The key to getting the kind of attendance that will make these signings worth your while is to remember that this is your book and your dream. Do not rely on the bookstore for publicity. Ask the store what their publicity plans are so that you do not duplicate their efforts. Then, you can go to work. The first thing you want to do is make your signing an "event." Create some excitement to draw the crowd. Create a topic for your event and develop promotional materials that you can send to the bookstores ahead of time, including counter-top posters and posters that can be placed in the window announcing your event. Develop postcard invitations that you can mail, have friends hand them out, or even have the stores distribute them to their customers. (You can have postcards developed with a picture of your book, leaving space for you to write in the information for each signing.)

Never underestimate the power of having friends and family attend your signings. Having a crowd gathered around you will draw other curious on-lookers. I suggest doing signings in cities where you have friends or family so you can have extra support in getting people to attend. Use any contacts you have to get media support¾feature articles, mentions in event calendars, etc. Signings preceded by media support are much more successful. Get a list of local media (newspapers, television, and radio) from the bookstores, then, send a press package to each contact, including the topic of your event, photos, time and other specifics. Remember, an "event" will be more appealing to the media than a "signing."

Once you're at the store, don't just sit behind a table. Be active in getting people to come and see what you have. People are attracted to activity. Make your event interesting.

If you follow these steps, you will win, the store will win, and you will be invited back. So, create and repackage yourself and have a great book event!

WOW! MY SELF-PUBLISHED BOOK IS BEING PICKED UP BY A MAINSTREAM PUBLISHER. CAN I RELAX NOW AND NOT BE CONCERNED ABOUT THE PUBLICITY?

WOW! MY SELF-PUBLISHED BOOK IS BEING PICKED UP BY A MAINSTREAM PUBLISHER. CAN I RELAX NOW AND NOT BE CONCERNED ABOUT THE PUBLICITY?

Dear Dr. Rosie,

I've had great success with my self-published non-fiction book. I've sold more than 10,000 copies in almost eight months. However, I am now looking into having my book picked up by a large publishing house so that I can relax and not be concerned about the publicity for my book. Is this a good idea?

Dear Author,

Congratulations on the success of your first book! You have shown that you are focused and determined. However, it sounds like you are suffering from what I call, "Author's Burn-out Syndrome." When attempting to decide regarding your writing and publishing future, you must revisit your motivation for writing in the first place. Let's look at a few reasons why writers write:

- They feel compelled to do so.

- They want the personal satisfaction of being published.

- They want to advance their cause.

- They want to share their knowledge.

- They want to advance their career.

- They want to earn a fortune.

The reason it is important to take another look at your motivation is that it will help you decide what to do if a major publisher does not give you a book deal.

Now, back to your original question, Is it a good idea to want to get published by a large publishing house so that you can relax and not be concerned with publicity? There is nothing wrong with wanting to be 'picked up' because there are many things that you can obtain with a larger publisher. However, publicity, promotion and marketing will still be something that you will very much have to be concerned with.

It is a fact that in today's publishing industry, the author is expected to take a very active role in helping to publicize their book. In editorial meetings, a frequently asked question is "Does the author have a platform?" This is especially true when publishers are evaluating the feasibility of a non-fiction project. How hard the author is willing to work on behalf of their book¾with public appearances, newspaper editorials, magazine columns, etc.—carry a great deal of weight when publishers are considering work for publication.

The bottom line is, there aren't any early retirement plans for the successful author. The book is always your business. It's like a partnership. You have to do more than show up for the camera and wait for royalty checks. In fact, if relaxing is your plan, it is more likely that you will never receive a royalty check, which could mean never getting another book deal.

Once again, look at your reasons for writing and remember there is no free ride in the publishing business.

I DO NOT HAVE THE FUNDS TO PUBLISH MY BOOK. IS "eBOOK" AN OPTION FOR GETTING MY BOOK ON THE MARKET?

I DO NOT HAVE THE FUNDS TO PUBLISH MY BOOK. IS "eBOOK" AN OPTION FOR GETTING MY BOOK ON THE MARKET?

Dear Dr. Rosie,

I've written a great novel and everyone who has read it tells me that it is excellent. In fact, all of my friends agree that they could not put it down. However, I have over 10 rejection letters from major publishers. Now, people are telling me to self-publish. I even heard that if I were to self-publish and sell thousands of books, I would have a better chance of being noticed by a major publisher and getting picked up. The challenge is, I don't have enough money to self-publish, but I have heard of something called an "eBook." Is this an option for getting my book into the market?

Dear Author,

Good question. eBook publishing is a viable option, but before I get into the benefits of e-publishing, let me address the point of getting noticed by a major house. It is true, in part, that some publishers may be more amenable to publishing books with authors who have some proven success. However, the writer must have good writing skills. There are several elements that go into a good novel, which include: a compelling plot, fully-developed characters and a story resolution. There are many writers who have great stories, however, writing good commercial fiction is a learned skill. Major publishers are seeking authors who already possess basic writing skills. Bottom line, the number of books you sell will not influence an editor's decision if your writing is not compelling and skillful.

There are publishing companies that offer book-packaging services, which include story-editing services. Story editing, which is different from copy editing can turn a good story into a great commercial novel. Also remember, rejections from publishing houses do not mean that your book is not good. Many commercial authors (who are successful today) were first widely rejected by mainstream publishers. Rejection did not discourage those authors¾many of them self-published and were then picked up by the same publishers who had rejected them before.

Now, the eBook question. It can be argued that the current publishing process helps screen out bad books by preventing them from reaching the marketplace, but the publishing industry is rife with stories of excellent books that can't get published and poor ones that do. The publication of eBooks moves the publication decision from the publisher to the author. One of the key points of eBook publishing is that it is a less-expensive method of getting your book into the market. However, no matter what method of publishing you choose, there are certain expenses you should never do without such as story editing and copy editing. (Note: a copy editor is concerned with spelling, grammar, and sentence structure, while a story editor's focus is on the story: pacing, dialogue, show versus tell, tension, and conflict, character development, etc.).

Obviously, e-Book publishing is less expensive because you're omitting the cost of printing. However, I would suggest that you have a cover for your book. That will give you a marketing edge. With eBooks you can reach a market that traditionally printed books have not reached, the visually impaired, and the literacy challenged. With eBooks, they have the opportunity to listen to stories.

So what is an eBook? Simply put, an e-Book is a special computer file, which contains the text of a printed book. The file may be read on a personal computer. One simply has to take the text of a book and convert it into a format usable by an e-Book reader. An eBook is simply data stored on a computer. The cost of storage and distribution is negligible compared with that of a printed book. Through the use of eBooks, it is more economically feasible to publish low demand titles. There are no shipping or handling charges when purchased online and books never go out of print. Also, authors have the ability to self-publish and distribute books inexpensively. eBooks may be downloaded quickly at home, or in a store via an Internet connection, making eBooks cost less than traditional books. No matter which route you choose, educate yourself thoroughly so you know what's right for you. Good luck!

Now that you have written your book, you will need a good understanding about your publishing options. The days are gone where authors have to be at the mercy of a mainstream publisher to get their book into the marketplace. New technology has made it simple for authors to get their books into the marketplace with the use of print-on-demand and E-Book publishing.

PRINT-ON-DEMAND: This makes publishing your book more financially feasible. You must still concern yourself with professionalism. Your book must be well written, properly edited, correctly formatted, and your cover must have great shelf impact. Presentation is the key regardless of the manner of publishing you choose. However, you do not have to come out-of-pocket for large print runs, having thousands of books in your garage. You can order and pay for books as you need them for yourself and as the customer demand is created from your marketing or via word-ofmouth. It does cost more for print-on-demand versus the cost per book if you printed 500-1,000 books with a conventional printer, but should you print less than 500 copies with a conventional printer, the cost per book will be more than the cost per book for print-on-demand. Until you create a large demand for your book, it's best to go with print-on-demand and leverage your finances. You can invest the difference into marketing and developing sales aides such as: postcards, bookmarkers, etc.

BOOKS: An eBook is electronically publishing your book. Some publishers will produce their electronic version of their book while they produce the printed version. Most mainstream publishing houses are publishing their books in ebook format also. After all, the new generation is reading and listening to their music on their iPod and other types of electronic devices. One can download an eBook using free programs such as Adobe Reader; however, not all eBooks are free. Some eBooks are priced the same as their printed version. We contend that an author should make his/her book available in every possible form to reach its full potential and to reach every market. Plus, the market of eBooks is growing. Our intent is to introduce you to the concept of E-Books to make it simpler for you. You can obtain information about eBooks on the Internet. Simply Google "eBooks.'

MY BOOK HAS BEEN REJECTED BY MAINSTREAM PUBLISHERS. ARE VANITY PUBLISHERS MY ONLY OPTION?

MY BOOK HAS BEEN REJECTED BY MAINSTREAMPUBLISHERS. AREVANITY PUBLISHERS MY ONLY OPTION?

Dear Dr. Rosie,

My book has been rejected by mainstream publishers. Are vanity publishers my only option?

Dear Author,

Let's take a close-up look at the publishing industry. The numbers are staggering. Every week, over 1,000 manuscripts cross the desks of New York publishers and editors, that's 52,000 manuscripts annually times multiple publishers. The average publishing house publishes 100 or less books per year; millions receive rejection letters. For the new or first-time author, these odds of being published by a mainstream publishing house can be disheartening.

Even when a book is "picked from the pack "to be published, over 90 percent of the newly published books do not sell out of their initial print run, which is usually 5,000 to 10,000 books.

Just looking at these facts and numbers could make an aspiring writer put down the pen, turn off the computer, and swear off writing forever! However, while these are the facts, it is possible to experience publishing success through proper planning and preparation.

The great thing about the publishing industry is that authors have choices. Today, authors have publishing options , which can ensure their book has a great chance for success. Authors simply have to choose the option, which works best for them. Here are three options available in publishing: Conventional or mainstream publishing, vanity/subsidy publishers, and selfpublishing.

Many writers can get frustrated quickly with this process and feel the need to enlist the services of a vanity publisher.

While mainstream publishers pay an author in advance for his/her book and pay for the total cost of publishing, vanity publishers are smaller companies that do not give advances to the author and who do not pay for the cost of production. Although the author owns the copyright, he/she must pay all costs associated with publishing the book. Vanity publishers are not your only option. In fact, some of these companies prey on those who have been rejected by mainstream publishers. They do not have to sell a single book to make a profit. You pay all the costs for the book, and then you have to buy your own book from them. On top of this, some vanity publishers receive a steep 60% commission on all books sold. In most cases, any great quantity of books sold will be those you sell yourself.

As an option you may want to consider self-publishing with the assistance of a publisher who provides book packaging services. These services include: book evaluation, editing, cover design, formatting, obtaining book credentials (ISBN numbers, bar codes, etc.) and printing. A professional book packaging company can give the self-published author a competitive edge by creating a product that will be sought out by mainstream publishers, if this is your aim, or a well-packaged product to market yourself.

www.ingramcontent.com/pod-product-compliance
Lightning Source LLC
Chambersburg PA
CBHW051839040426

42447CB00006B/608